DIRT BIKES

MARYSA STORM

**BLACK
RABBIT
BOOKS**

Bolt Jr. is published by Black Rabbit Books
P.O. Box 3263, Mankato, Minnesota, 56002.
www.blackrabbitbooks.com
Copyright © 2020 Black Rabbit Books

Michael Sellner, designer; Omay Ayres, photo researcher

Names: Storm, Marysa, author.
Title: Dirt bikes / by Marysa Storm.
Description: Mankato, Minnesota : Black Rabbit Books,
[2020] | Series: Bolt Jr. Wild rides | Includes bibliographical
references and index. | Audience: Age 6-8. | Audience:
K to grade 3.
Identifiers: LCCN 2019001760 (print) | LCCN 2019002399
(ebook) | ISBN 9781623101923 (e-book) |
ISBN 9781623101862 (library binding) |
ISBN 9781644661185 (paperback)
Subjects: LCSH: Trail bikes–Juvenile literature.
Classification: LCC TL441 (ebook) | LCC TL441 .S76 2020
(print) | DDC 629.227/5–dc23
LC record available at https://lccn.loc.gov/2019001760

Printed in the United States. 5/19

Contents

CHAPTER 1

A Wild Ride

Dirt bikes race around a track. Their **knobby** tires kick up dirt. The riders speed toward a jump. Then they launch into the air. The bikes land with a thud. They continue down the track.

knobby: having bumps

dirt bike tire ◄ · · · · · · · · · · · · · ·

narrow and bumpy

COMPARING
· · · · · **TIRES** · · · ·

Speedy and Strong

Dirt bikes are built for off-road riding.
They have tough frames and tires.
Dirt bikes can handle rough landings.
They speed over jumps. They zip
through turns.

▶ **sport bike tire**
wide and smooth

PARTS OF A
Dirt Bike

exhaust pipes

tires

8

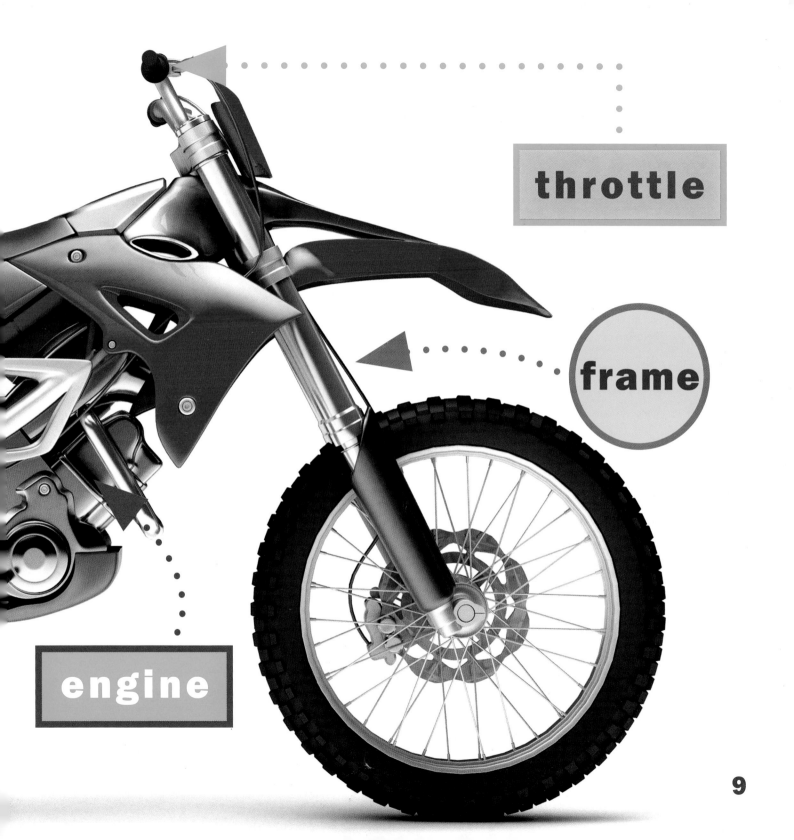

throttle

frame

engine

CHAPTER 2

Different Types

Not all dirt bikes are the same. Riders use **enduro** bikes for long races. The bikes have big gas tanks. Riders race **motocross** bikes on rough tracks. The bikes are light but tough.

enduro: a long race

motocross: the sport of racing bikes over a rough course

FACT

Enduro races can last days.

Trail and Dual-Sport

Riders use trail bikes on trails. The bikes aren't very fast. They're more comfortable. **Dual**-sport bikes have lights and mirrors. Riders can use them on regular roads.

dual: having two different parts

13

Popular Motocross Tracks

Spring Creek,
United States

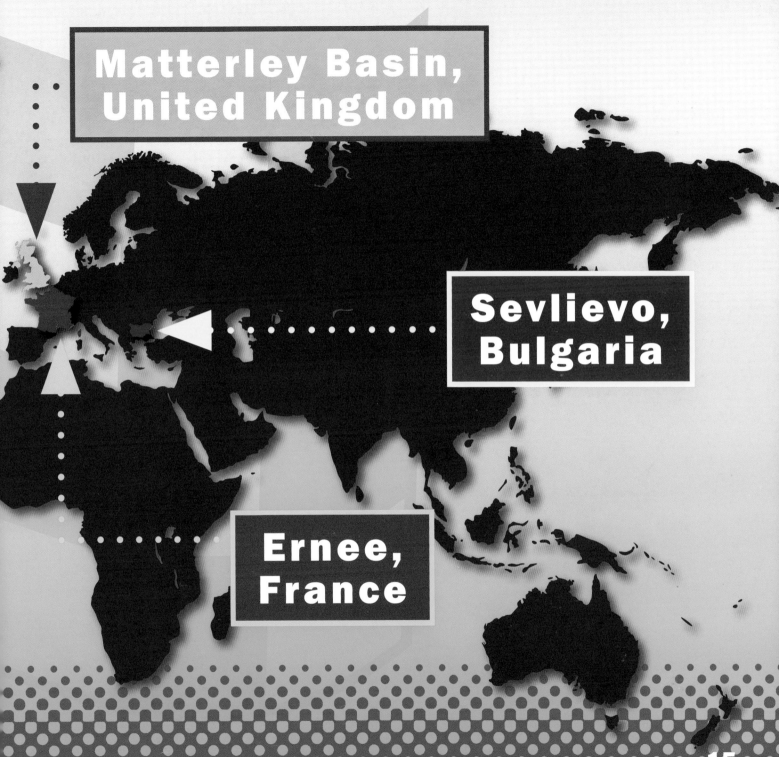

Matterley Basin, United Kingdom

Sevlievo, Bulgaria

Ernee, France

CHAPTER 3

Racing On

Dirt bike racing began in the 1900s. The bikes have changed a lot since then. They now have many plastic parts. Plastic makes them lighter. Lighter bikes are faster.

FACT

The first motocross race happened in 1924.

Fast and Fun

Future bikes might be even lighter. They would be even faster. New materials might make them stronger. No matter what, they'll stay super fun.

· · · · · · · · · · · · · · **Average Dirt Bike Weight**
about 200 pounds
(91 kilograms)

19

Bonus Facts

Riders brake using their right hands and feet.

Riders can do **amazing tricks.**

People began using plastic parts in the 1950s.

Riders wear **safety** gear.

gear: supplies, tools, or clothes used for a special purpose

21

READ MORE/WEBSITES

Katirgis, Jane, and James Holter. *Racing Dirt Bikes.* Speed Racers. New York: Enslow Publishing, 2018.

Schuh, Mari. *The Motorcycle Race.* Let's Race. Mankato, MN: Amicus Readers, Amicus Ink, 2017.

Shaffer, Lindsay. *Dirt Bikes.* Full Throttle. Minneapolis: Bellwether Media, Inc., 2019.

Dirt Bike
www.motorcycle-usa.com/dirt-bike/

Dirt Bike Riding Tips
www.dirtbikeschool.org/safety.aspx

Motocross 101
www.kidzworld.com/article/6121-motocross-101

GLOSSARY

dual (DOO-uhl)— having two different parts

enduro (in-DUR-oh)—a long race

gear (GEER)—supplies, tools, or clothes used for a special purpose

knobby (NOB-ee)—having bumps

motocross (MOH-toh-kraws)—the sport of racing bikes over a rough course

INDEX